BLUESTOWN MOCKINGBIRD

Mambo

Sandra María Esteves

Arte Público Press
Houston
Texas
1990

Aknowledgements

This book is made possible by a grant from the National Endowment for the Arts, a federal agency.

Selected poems from this book first appeared in the following:

"Mambo Love Poem" first appeared in *Areito* Vol.8, No.29; Ediciones Vitral, Inc., G.P.O. Box 1913, New York, NY 10116, 1982; and subsequently produced by Angela Flemming/WNYC-TV video poetry series, 1 Centre St., New York, NY 10007, 1989.

"From The Ferrybank," in *Hanging Loose 52*'; Hanging Loose Press, 231 Wyckoff St., Brooklyn, NY 11217, 1988.

"Love Affair With A Welfare Hotel," in *Centro Bulletin*, Spring '88, Centro de Estudios Puertorriqueños; Hunter College, City University of New York, 695 Park Ave, New York, NY 10021, 1988.

"Fighting Demons," in *Art Against Apartheid: Works For Freedom*, IKON Inc., P.O. Box 1355, Stuyvesant Station, New York, NY 10009, 1986.

Arte Público Press
University of Houston
Houston, Texas 77204-2090

Esteves, Sandra María, 1948–
Bluestown Mockingbird Mambo / Sandra Maria Esteves.
p. cm.
ISBN 1-55885-017-1
1. Puerto Ricans—New York (N.Y.)—Poetry   I. Title.
PS3555.S825B55 1990
811'.54–dc20

90-193
CIP

Photo by Evangelina Vigil-Piñón

The following precious verses

are dedicated

to Lela,

Ife, Cristina, Yaasmiyn, Alia,

and Shamsul,

with all my love.

Table of Contents

3. Batarumba Autonomy

BLUESTOWN MOCKINGBIRD MAMBO

1

Indian Solo

Affirmations #1, Life Shopping in Ma Becksy's Deli

When I open my heart ta sing,
I read poems for life.
An' it works like warm creole brewin'
where the soul can breathe and be,
that's where these words live.

Not no poems for no frozen metaphors,
nor for no pains been achin' too long.
Got nothin' for no peddlers ain't doin'
nothin' for no dead space in my head.
Solicitin' emptiness is not on my shopping list.

Don't have no praises of glory for all the times
I bin shot down for bein' woman, or simple,
or brown skin, talkin' Bronx.

I can only state my celebrations
over the greyness of the wallpaper
where ivy roots an acid anchor into cement.

Poems are for the livin', that's what I know.
An' if I could sing and dance,
grow greens in my backyard,
I'd be livin' poetry from sunrise ta sunset,
an' all the chaos in between.

Natural combustion.
Greenpoems, colorpoems, rootpoems,
to-curl-yr-mind-in-space-poems.
Is good cookin'.

... Now when they tell me ta come up wif some taylor made,
I go all in thru my file cabinets
ta find me some seeds a rebellion.
Catchin'-up-wif-myself I call it,
for clearin' up the air,
burn thru sleep/thick clouds.
Sift thru endless sheets of used yellow legal,
findin' old quotes from the graveyard,

ta remind my sensitive perspectives ta come clean wif myself.
See just how much reality I can take on at one time.
How much of the whole is me?
How much am I a reflection?
Rich glasses of water wearin' grass.
No middlemen, or research analysts,
no statisticians, or multispecial mentalists.
Just bein', growin', livin'.

Smoothpoems I learn from the earth
an' movement of the sungod
that gave it's heart to the sacrifice
in occult folkloric media events.

And within these verses is history,
since before the age of many-hued-man,
even before that ol' wives' tale 'bout some woman
an' some man's rib.
I tell you, these folkloric pictures must be questioned.
Tis' a prism mind the eye becomes.
For ta grow, ya got ta keep growin'.

... So I reviewed the purchase order in mind,
and made suggestions on the selection of the fabric,
'cause two cents is always worth somethin' ta me.
An' found poems fittin' snug,
jazzy an' rainbow, I tell you,
it was truly worth the metamorphose,
people wondering why they exist,
workin' ta make the best of it,
wearin' completeness like a new set a wings,
beyond dimensions of their expectations,
a marvelous creation, real live peoplepoems,
forming circles around their fire-wind.

Autobiography of A Nuyorican

for Lela

Half blue, feet first
she battled into the world.
Hardly surviving the blood cord twice wrapped,
tense around her neck. Hanging.
Womb pressing, pushing,
pulling life from mother's child.
Fragil flesh emerging perfect in blueness,
like the lifeline that sustained her,
yet limp, almost a corpse.

Her mother claims the virgin interceded.
Invoked through divine promise, in prayer,
that caused her dark eyes to open,
her tongue to taste air like fire,
as the blueness faded,
tracing death on the tail of an eclipse.

And as in birth from her darkness,
the free-giving sun inched slow to visibility,
revealing all color and form,
a great teacher, generous and awesome,
silent and reverent, loud and blasphemous,
constant,
sculpting edges of definition
in the shadow and light of multiple universes.

Half blue, feet first
she battled her way.
The world did not want another brown,
another slant-eyed-olive-indian-black-child.
Did not want another rainbow empowered song
added to repertoire in blue,
or azure, or indigo,
or caribbean crystal.
Did not want another mouth to feed,
especially another rock-the-boat poet,
another voice opened wide,

fixed on a global spectrum of defiance.

The meaning of war defined her. Gasping and innocent,
before she knew her mother,
before she discovered herself, barely alive,
gathering weapons into her being with each breath that filled her,
growing stronger,
determined
to beat all the odds.

Springfield

Successful stockbroker's live-in maid,
in the fifties Ina worked,
alternating weeks between stylish mid-manhattan co-op
and fifteen-hundred-acre connecticut farm,
five miles from her mama's house.

Her six year old godchild's first summer out
got to ride the limo, next to Godmother'
respectful behind her employers.
An hour later she threw up, car sick.
Their luxurious back seat stinking.
After that, she always rode the bus.

Just off main street
Ma Becksy's second floor flat
over a miller's store.
Back porch stairs leading
to a backyard feast of explorations.

The abandoned barn housed newsprint
like giant sentries on call.
She'd sneak in through wallboard spaces
large enough for a small child's crawl.
Play hide-and-seek, tag, with the watchman.

Spent sunny days wandering down the road,
barely one-block stretch of sidestreet,
into crabapple orchards,
a forest mile of natural wonders
between the dead end and the high school.
Crushing fallen green fruit into applesauce carpets.
Recovering branches to go fishing in the mosquito pond.
Catching lily pads, pretended they were big tuna.

Country civilization no bigger than two city blocks.
Firehouse, police station, library,
greasy spoon bus stop, dry goods stores.
The first time she met regular town's folks, they all stared.
Godmother explained they never saw one like her before,

indian-haired-mulata-puerto-rican-girl.
Only knew black and white, nothing inbetween.

The corner shop used to sell fashion tailored suits.
A year later became bric-a-brac antiques and old books.
Twenty-five cents bought her first library.
A nine volume treasure she could not even read.
But thumbed through each page,
hunting pictures to explain mysterious words,
claiming possession of knowledge with ownership.

Twenty-five cents of intelligence went a long way.
Already smarter, even without pictures.
Could make out letters ... M ... A ... Z ... E ...
Proud of lightweight abilities,
thought she understood the world.

Examined the last of the books on the courthouse steps.
Satisfied to have absorbed their contents,
left them behind for another curious buyer.

Took afternoon naps in Godmother's double bed,
drifting to sleep watching spiders weaving window corners.
Sometimes wake to one curious bug
hanging face-to-face from low country ceiling,
making her feel like an intruder before she'd scream.

Later she'd watch Godmother
picking fresh mint for Ma Becksy.
She let her smell it once.
So anxious to please, the child went mint picking too,
sniffing every bush in sight till she found the right one.

Doc yelled at Ina for trusting ghetto-kid wisdom.
Ma Becksy almost died from the tea it made.
After that, she never hunted mint leaves again.

Father's Day On Longwood Avenue

for Charlie

Returning to that abandoned past of youth,
Bronx neighborhood of her father's house.
A five story structure, still, but standing.
Where once his tall husky frame sat
in a top floor window, drinking beer.
As she watched from below,
in awe of this person, she barely knew.

Three blocks south from him
the Beck Street tenament she first claimed home,
last year, torn to the ground.
Nineteen years tumbled into shadows,
dust traces of rubble remain,
names of neighbors, best friends, disappeared.

And in the place where her room once held her,
where she became alive, cried,
and learned to love her mother,
studying world through windows facing sun,
chanting incantations to the Moon
of top forty hit parades
in fourth floor ghetto repertoire.
Space of broken concrete, limping paint,
so dear, the only water she knew,
now a lane through a park where lover's walk
over new matted rugs of prefabricated astroturf.
While memories of building linger in trees,
Titi Julia's apartment one, where life began,
now air and space where birds fly in symbolic liberation
of land reclaimed by wind,
spirit of her home set free,
an unraveled karma.

While the shell of her father's house endures,
a monument braced against the elements.
Roof leaking to basement, only rats take notice.
Winds howling lonely sonatas, no one hears.

A single pigeon flies west, silhouetting sunset.
She remembers a young woman of thirteen
looking for the last time
at this stranger not seen for twenty-six years,
wondering
who he was.

Sistas

Nina Simone, Celia Cruz, Billy Holiday, and Bessie
were all her sistas growin' up,
keepin' her company through only-child-blues.
Afternoons spent laughin', cryin', dancin' motown gold,
harmonizin' are-'n-be teen sweet melodies.

Aretha Franklin, La Lupe, Diana and the Supremes
stayed up nights at heartbreak hotel,
rappin' real close moonshine doo-waps,
patiently riffin' their lines till she learned all the words.
Takin' it higher,
hittin' all the notes home.

Ronnie Scepter and Gladys Knight hung out too.
The first time ever she heard Roberta Flack,
knew they were fruit from the same feelin' tree.
How they loved her madly without even tryin'.
Didn't have to be nobody. Didn't need to prove.
They never got tired, or complained about the volume,
or even cared who was listenin'.
Always by her side, no matter what.
Tight for days.
Gettin' it on. Gettin' down.

Sistas all the way.

I Want To Paint

Recreate life on an empty surface.
Place myself in a rainforest of tropical jubilation, cool and
     moist.
Meditate on textures of shaded mist,
dripping over primary renditions of dream tones.
Flash a large stroke of sunburst across a never ending rain.

I want to paint, the way Betty Carter can deliver a blues
like you've always wanted to hear it.
The way Andy Gonzalez makes his base race
over a syncopated turnpike.
The way Thulani and Ntosake dialogue woman tunes
within the hearts of poems.
The way Louis Reyes Rivera breaks a casual word
into one hundred songs.

I want to paint.
Become the canvass, the walls,
the brushes and colors,
pens, pencils, and fine line markers.
Be the shapes and shadows, the highlights and reflections,
the dominant emotions of all my strokes.

I want to wear combinations in my hair
of dawn, caribbean ocean, rainbow,
mountain jungle, noon day sun, moon lit night,
the chaos and the calm,
a fire breathing dragon shooting a golden blaze,
a supersonic jet across a clear sky,
a volcano.

I want to fill my landscapes
with trees, rivers, thunderstorms, mountains,
dirt roads along fields of flower-scented grass,
build bridges across oceans,
hold up my half of the sky with the palms of these hands.

I want to paint. Be
the sounds that make me come alive,

even when they make me cry,
recreate this pattern of existence,
bringing forth the birth of our own voices,
bursting with the melodies of our own songs

—then, I want to listen to them ...
... as they sing.

Religious Instructions For Young Casualties

Believe in yourself.
Be all that you can.
Look for your fate among the stars.
Imagine you are your best when being yourself
the best way you can.

Believe in yourself. Be all you want to be.
Open your mind, a window to the world,
different ways of thinking, seeing,
but be yourself—it's the best.

Become your dreams, visions to live by.
No matter what anyone says,
believe you can do it.
Day by day, a little at a time.
Be patient.

Believe you can find a way
to assemble the puzzle called life,
forming pictures that make some kind of sense.
Even when pieces fall scattered to the ground,
disappearing into the finite void,
forever lost, never to be found,
choosing your future from those that are left,
like one piece from some other dimension.

Maybe a corner triangle shape of sky,
or zigzag of ocean floor with seaweed and one school of fish,
or maybe a centerpiece on the table in some fancy dining
        room,
or patch of window lace curtain next to flowered bouquet,
wind blowing through sunlight, which some artist will paint
        someday.
Or bouncing feet on the moon,
walking in giant moon leaps, talking moon talk,
deep into research in your flying laboratory.

Be all that you can, but believe in yourself.
Climb the stairway of your imagination, one step after an-

other.
Growing like the leaf, blossoming into a great tree,
complete with squirrels, nests, universe all around.

Be all that you can,
just believe in yourself.

Mambo Love Poem

Carlos y Rebecca dance across the floor.
They move in mambo cha-cha
that causes the sweat of their bodies to swirl
in a circle of tropical love.

Carlos y Rebecca move
and the room fills with blazes of red.
Flaming pianos breezing spicy tunes as coconuts fall
from palm trees ancient to these children.
As coconuts fall from imaginary palm trees
ancient to Borinquen souls.
Imaginary coconuts fall to the beat of their feet
in rhythm with the talking African drum.

Rebecca y Carlos glide across the floor,
and two become one in the land of salsa.
The sweat of their bodies mingles with flute
blowing high over splintered wooden floors,
in notes that soar beyond the rooftops of El Barrio.

They forget their pain in this land of joy,
as the clave answers the singing African conga,
the dancing African drum,
the conga quintiando
the African tongue.
Rebecca y Carlos become one
like two birds flying through the open sky,
in mambo cha-cha to celebrate their joy,
their feet no longer touching the ground.

They dance
becoming jíbaros in eagle wings.
As Shangó—Cabio Sile—enters their bodies
their sweat fuses with light.
Like thunderbolts in a fiery desert,
great wings galloping in flight.
The light in their feet dancing the African beat
with the singing African drum,
the conga quintiando the African tongue.

Marking the warrior's rhythm with the singing dancing drum,
Shangó—Cabio Sile—enters their bodies,
they flow magically into one.

Mother's Day At Doña Rodríguez

for Aya

We never met, but I knew her.
By that ray of life passed into her son,
brilliant as sky through cane fields,
casting pastel shadows on a jíbaro's balcón,
abundant fruit and flower scented
from an ancient caribbean, full of spirit
y la vida india.

I never heard her cry, but I was there,
at the birth, when the hurricane growled,
fierce and terrible, screaming,
as she listened to its thunder within herself,
her womb stretching,
pushing out the manchild she offered the world,
not in regret, but full
of remembrances, of land-plowing farmers,
plátano covered rainforests,
asphalt paths carved in slavery
through migrant jungles and concrete mountains.

I never saw the high curve of her taíno face
with its delicate brown cheek,
or felt the caress of her motherly hands. But I knew her,
recognized in emanating points of vision
from a craftmaker's fingertips,
in precision woven tapestries, like gifts from ancestors,
marking borderlines where families become whole.

We never spoke, or shared a conversation,
but I can still hear the music
composed in the black latino brew of her kitchen.
Smells and leftover renditions of creole beans and salsa,
of mamá-cooking ladles tapping three/two clave
from sinks to pots to laundry machines
in survival ritual symphonies.

We never exchanged a word,

yet she whispered to my soul,
the way mother teaches son to love his child,
the way father shares with daughter the meaning of abuela,
the way bonds are secured
like a sunday afternoon banquet at the table of Orisha
where all food is nourished,
love-seasoned.

I never knew her, yet she reached out,
as sister, woman, teacher,
as mother, a gentle wind,
touching me. Becoming mine.

Invisible Inscriptions

María and Roberto were lovers once.
If you could describe their ambivalence in such a way.
Come-in-closer-
    but-stay-away politics.
Love-me-but-don't-get-attached-
    I-won't-be-around-tomorrow syndrome.
I-just-want-to-check-you-out-for-a-minute-
    a-second-will-do maneuver.
Let-me-see-your-ass-and-I'll-know-
    if-I-want-to-stay-or-not strategy.

Roberto was full of illusions,
insights into impossible fantasies.
In their house the high strung wind blew one direction,
fierce, untamed, vicious,
a ruthless note of mental mutiny,
no kinship or connected identity,
just broken promises of imitation fruit.

María grew, even if only from the wisdom of critique.
Learning to hold back, instead,
offer alternatives,
vowing to fight in the war
where there are no uniforms,
only weapons of peace to master,
wiping permanent scars along the way
from the photographs of her past,
working to overcompensate the shift in trajectory
pulling her constantly out of orbit
by the speeding bullet of Roberto's insanity.

On feb 19th a part of her died.
She now speaks from this grave.
The marker reads wife, a bold title in flat letters.
No names are attached here,
only the shell of what is left when all else has been removed,
a testament of complete and brutal rejection
of this self and her giving,

of darkness lit by a passing sun,
of words scraped from inside the abyss
where an instant of vision reveals time reversed.
What was, no longer is.
What is, comes to nothing.

A murder has been committed.
There was no shedding of blood, no outcry
to warn the neighbors,
no calculated resistances
or possibilities for choice,
just random cold stares, unexpected shockwaves,
storms of violent undertones,
a surprise ending of empty harvest.

There was not even a burial
to praise the worthy. In fact,
nothing to indicate the presence of death,
but smouldering embers,
now searching definition in the poetry of these words,
images crying out from ashes,
with all that is left after theft of dignity.
Fragil remnants.
Pieces of rare moments to fill a life,
to conceive refreshment on the road
where we shall all meet our destiny,

In spite of it all,
within herself
María finds the only secure place,
the universe of her thoughts
to guide her forward,
to rise taller into her being,
tapping the dynamic power of rebirth,
discovering the metaphor of her dreams,
the maker of visions for herself to become.

Rites of Passage #1, María Poeta Bled Daily

Escaping into her art,
restless words fashioned from political voids,
bleeding tears on pages seeking hope,
soiled afterthoughts,
daily conspiracies of masked friendships,
desperately clingling to meaningless routines,
structures simulating empty existences,
encountering frustration, anxiety, disappointment
as she searched for heaven
through littered street gardens,
trying to pray by the sacred ocean,
finding, not golden silence, but demon sounds,
misbegotten assassins, stalking,
spitting, foaming, offering dead life,
weighing her.

Yet with all that, she wanted a career.
She wanted to order aspirations and ideals
the way she could fold up laundry,
freshly washed underwear,
to emerge sweet smelling and warm,
conditioned, neatly stacked on the closet shelf.

There were almost no choices.
Only continuous betrayal by the englishized accents
of the unspoken Indian language in her soul.
She had to mount investigations
into corners hiding answers,
wanting to feel no shame about herself,
living honest,
creating visions the way God produced universes
transforming before her eyes
miracles that walked and breathed,
flowers she bloomed, barely two pounds,
fiercely grasping life,
commanding her own,
to be powerful as sun,
her radiance holding balance,

orbiting perfect revolutions,
bringing forth roses from the rain,
a guidebook of edible language for her children.

So Your Name Isn't María Cristina

for Luz María Umpierre

All right. I'll accept that.
She was just a young woman. Another Puertorriqueña among
    many.
Desperate to define self within worlds of contradictions.
Caught somewhere inbetween the casera traditions of Titi
    Julia
and the progressive principles of a Young Lords cousin.

I'll admit she was barely a child, with no definitions of her
    own.
No recognition of her vast cultural inheritance.

She didn't used to know herself.
Having to pick and choose from surrounding reflections.
Needing alternatives to focus by.
So she found them here and there,
tried them on for size and feeling,
taking pieces from different places,
coordinated like a wardrobe,
sometimes elegant, most times plain.

María Cristina was naive when she wrote her first poem,
just beginning her metamorphosis,
struggling for explanations in the complications of being,
searching her unique place in the world, purpose for exis-
    tence.
Discovering new meanings for old words
listed in the encyclopedia of colonialism.
Each day becoming reference volumes,
forming bridges of correspondence from old to new worlds.

She's not young anymore, not like before.
Anyone can change.
In fact, she's become someone else since those old times,
even though her name is still the same.

So your name isn't María Cristina,
but it really doesn't matter in which barrio you were born.

We all get the same kick in the ass
by faces that are similar.
You're still her older sister, teacher of many metaphors.
When she was ignorant you pulled her closer,
explaining the fruits of your experiences.
She watched how you fixed your own faucets,
defending yourself against heartless violations.
How you marked out your path with defiant resistance
against all forms of enslavement.
How you fought, yelled back,
at those who wanted you to fail, expected it, crossing you.
She watched it all, and learned from the watching
that weeding the garden is constant to its cultivation.

It's a good thing you were around.

Now she can build her own house
as well as sew, cook, wash, have babies,
even if her name hasn't changed.

So your name isn't María Cristina,
but you forgot to tell me if you understood
she was just one person,
one Borinqueña within our universal identity.
In some ways a lot like Titi Julia
who took care of her when Mami went to work.
You remember her, don't you?

The point is she grew,
and watched, and studied, and learned,
awakening into womanhood.

But María Cristina isn't a little girl anymore.
Everything came the hard way,
like breathing and walking the first time.
Self perception took time to evolve into new values,
to patiently believe in her possibilities.

Now she can build her own house,
even though her name hasn't changed.

Thank God,
it was a good thing you were around.

Native American

for Beti

If I am tree
then I am of fallen leaf, dissolved and dead,
decayed deep into earth,
covered by ancient crust of time,
beaten centuries of inheritance, a seed,
barren, but reaching to become
the new tree.

And if I am of tree
then this is the one I am, for none other could I be.

And if I am of leaf of fallen seed
then I am of wood that carved Arsenio's guitar,
that plucks strings pulsating messages
discovered before the adventurer Columbus,
in a bloodstream covering five continents, connected
under the sunlight of heaven.

And if I am of tree, then what is my name?
García, González, Jiménez, Rodríguez,
Puente, Palmieri, Figueroa, Santamaría,
Cordero, Corea, Quintana, Baretto,
Santana, Quarionex, Agüeybana Cemí?
Who is this precious person, living, breathing,
wanting to be, inside of me?

And how does my bark heal?
For what was it meant to be?
What type is this tree?
Will I be a tall grand evergreen like the greatest, Mohammed
   Ali?
Branches spreading wide green bristles full of trophies.
Or will I grow sweet and sour apples in some fine country
   orchard
worried only of the unexpected frost,
forever blooming every doctor's remedy?
Or some exotic fruit? Peach, pineapple, coconut,

papaya, mango, kiwi seed,
wide leafed banana tree,
plantain, avocado, brown black coffee bean,
picked by a hardly-paid-a-dime migrant worker,
fated for some fast-foods breakfast store–
please, may my fate this not be.

Will I be hidden on the side of a mighty mountain
somewhere in the heart of Indian land
where sparrow speaks to crow
deciphering clouds to forcast the day?

Or will I be burned by some careless camper's fire?
Will lightening strike me down?
Will I live forever like the giant California redwood?
How high will I climb? What sights will I see?
Will I be rooted in a meadow, a lucious distant valley,
or stuck cold to die on a merciless city street?

Will I live in a field fascinated by my variety,
short, tall, wide, thin?
Will my leaves fall yellow-orange, red-maple, green?
Will I burn in someone's fireplace and bring in warmth?
Or be the surrounding protecting wall
of a house? Or some tower of distinction?
Or a chair? Or a table? Or a bed? Or a pencil?
Or the page of a guilded book many will read,
opening doors to other dimensions ...

Afterbirths

for Elsie

Images of women come in multiple shades.
Tints and lights of prism-fractured textures
forming semi-precious facets,
opaque, clear, crystalline,
capturing color blends of unrecorded histories,
invisible, from all points around the mountain,
emanating bleeding river veins stretching to the sea,
reflecting endless temperaments of sky
under canopy of stars revealing new secrets.

Images of women are formed sharing the same names,
goddess, whore, daughter, sister, misfit, friend,
teacher.
Images of hands holding onto children, carrying them
in their arms, on their backs, over their hips,
forever swimming through oceans of tears,
with barely a bowl of grain for planting,
transforming barren origins into orchards of fruit gardens.

Ordinary women enduring, taking control of their lives,
survivors in triumph over self,
claiming victory with bodies scarred and puffed
from passage rites through the childbirth wars,
persuing meaning and purpose, committed,
determined to make a difference.

Cooking, clothes washing, factory working,
red-white-blue collared women,
juxtaposed and holding onto each other,
embracing life,
finding knowledge through their being together,
always the mother, often the martyr,
continuously willing to give.

Affirmations #2, There Is A Poet Inside You

Let the muse come out.
Give her space to speak her name
crying to be heard.

How she sees through visible indifference.
Her sharp eye an architect's pen, electric,
deciphering cosmic symphonies,
on a mission,
beautiful as air, shaping wind,
a carpenter's knife edged in rays of light,
soft, fire blue, barely a horizon.

This Is A Hill That Climbs

A gradual rise towards a turbulent horizon.
A sancturary for strayed eagles,
with feathers oil drenched and refinery wearied.

This is a canyon cut of stone.
Within growing layers of time revealed,
a bloodstream of tears from where the proud are born.

This is a river which smooths the surface of rock.
Wearing down the crusted mountain skin
that divides the earth of freedom from the sea of misery.

This is a sky of restless motion.
Born of thunder as it moves towards it's destiny,
preparing for the coming rain.

This is a silent haven. Dancing deliverance
played within a mental confine,
speaking to itself in the language of soul.

This is a rainfall washing fertility dust.
A reservoir of godbreath, pollen of potential,
seeds, trees, victory garden orchards.

This is a hill that climbs continuously upwards.
Awaiting the final descent, the inevitable alchemy
into the valley of eternity.

This is a tree that is seen for miles.
Upon which come the winged
to build their nests.

This is a hill rising from the earth.
A swollen breast
suckling her children,

adorning their crowns with great feathers,
peacock and phoenix,
wild mockingbird.

2

For Immediate Delivery

Love Affair With A Welfare Hotel

A city breeds corruption.
Abundant,
like a dripping faucet,
spilling a payload of drug blood
into gutters where children play,
watching pushers
pushing nightmares into their dreams.

No money for wood and nails,
or for building new foundations.
No money for books, or pencils,
just enough to fill the coffers of greedy lords
who wait by desks that register the homeless.

While in Guatemala
fifty thousand dreams are shattered
into shades, shapes of fine glass
cut sharp, irregular.
Families dissipated into refugee camps,
severed from their roots,
replanted in artificial gardens
where no one has a name,
and nothing is known
but the interest rate
produced by slaves of the neonazichristianrepublicanstates
in the war that never ends.

What gives them the right
to displace a people from their land,
destroy traditions built up over centuries,
redefine the borderline of priorities,
imposed, dictated, and controlled?

In Guatemala
you cannot call your brother in Santa Monica,
take a spin in your corvette,
shop roosevelt field on sunday afternoons,
eating meat at least once a day.

In Guatemala
fifty thousand hopes for a future
wait for directions to the next relocation center
while others flee into jungles,
willing to die for their liberation.

Puerto Rican Discovery #5, Here Like There

Chaos spills over from another era
they had no part in the making.

Weeds appear from remote corners
only the sun notices. A world evolves
busily ignoring its own blinded sight.
Songs from Managua hit in counterbalance,
geometrically perpendicular to stone forests,
petrified like soldiers fearing the unknown.

An infant gun creates a canyon of history
exploding paths into oblivion,
searching split-seconds of focus into its birth,
a hurricane gnarled and twisted,
sheltering a brooded following,
demanding attention on a world stage.
Insisting space, a voice in its own house.

Like there in Puerto Rico,
mountains and sea wage vain attempts
to purify the plastic layer
breathless and tight over its victim,
a flag stuffed luscious,
laying to rot in ambivalent warehouses
of aborted children
from an indifferent
                    ... mother.

Alternative Points of View

for Liz

1.

You phone them,
all threatening,
demanding to speak to your ex-husband,
father of your two sons.

You call,
harassing your way through communication lines,
delivering profanity like marbles in your mouth,
crying falsetto blues.
Poor choices for a mother of kings.

You call,
like mistress
in heat for a fix,
that never comes.
Desperate.
Searching that fountain of youth.
Leaving your dignity nodding on corners,
cracking the walls of your house,
cursing your children.
Betrayed by a fast trick to nowhere.

Like a thief in the night
you set up your prey.
Spinning that sinister snare.
The bait, your two sons,
taking turns begging.

You call.
Missing words
of how you love yourself,
are wanting to create gardens in your window,
providing nourishment. Many levels.
Singing praises.
Teaching your sons the meaning of becoming gods.

2.

Two sons, two brothers.
Shamsul, the sword, sage of sun.
Hakim, the knower, the guide.
Partners on an unknown course.
Destiny begotten of light.
Small beauty becoming great.
Intelligence and feelings forming alliances for seeing.
Trying to make it, day by day.

Unprescribed Symptoms Of A Life Withdrawal

A puff of betrayal disguised in Judas kisses.
A snort of hatred multiplied by opportunism.
A bag of foolishness smoked through a pipe of abandon-
    ment.
An etheral race ten times light speed rushing to a night-
    mare.
An incoherent phone call,
rambling through a dialogue of deception.
A needle of death courting ill vision.
A drink of fire in a straw house.
A sea foam spitting vengeance.
A rabid desire for a fresh kill of leg.
A two-faced friend masked in envy.
A greed of endless proportions.
A viper sucking a poisoned heart smothered,
swallowed whole into a vast lonely temple.

Another soldier crucified.

3:00 A.M. Eulogy For A Small Time Poet

for M. P.

I will not mourn for you my friend,
or allow death to steal my tears.
Nor bend to pain. Sharing sympathy to mockery on parade.
Nor sorrow for the dead. Nor the living dead.
Nor the living who hunger for death.
Nor bring blooms to the graves of child molestors.

These are not the concerns of angels or gods.
But of fallen angels and false gods.
Feelings too precious for waste,
but saved to nourish future souls,
hundreds who kissed the point of your dagger,
rejoicing release in your demise
in this hour of consumption.
Now free dancing, naked
in the silk white veil of their being,
not fearing your hidden shadow
making victims of their love,
nor entrapped by the tendersweet poison of your voice,
fanged.

No,
I will not mourn for you my friend.

Though there are many
who in this moment do.

Original Jones Poem In B♭

for Américo Casiano

Dime high craving blue acid.
Miami-vice systematic syndrome.

Ounce high in three ton panic clave.
Blues craze in puke red medley.

Quick high leaping head.
Ice cool freeze. Numb dead.

Drunk high daring dissipated dense.
Self-centered distant nerve endings.

Syncopated madness on a psychedelic curve.
Simulated fulfillment of temporary realization.

Bastard hopes orphaned by suicidal fantasies.
Self inflicted trauma

orchestrated in community plague.
Memoirs in abuse mode

cryin' jazz in cold storage alto.
Snatching half-tones of sensation.

Flying high on laid back horny downbeats.
Chillin' on death, the ultimate orgasm.

Forgetting
to just say no.

South Bronx Testimonial #3, We Are All Insane

In this eternal dance,
drinking a polluted nectar,
breathing a poisoned air,
humming a disjointed tune in disoriented melody.

We create chaos. Wallow in it.
Market it,
the way the food is tampered.

We are all hopelessly, blindly, incurably insane.
Staring at each other from pseudo facades,
pretending to be immune to the plague of lunacy,
yelling irrelevant incoherences at our selves.

We have lost our freedoms,
to walk barefoot over the earth
without stepping on dubious manufactured chemicals
guaranteed to produce plastic lawn,
or dip in the ocean without catching slime,
or sing from the mountain, watching sun
without seeing one rooftop antenna,
wanting to play outdoors, not worried
about getting kidnapped,
or molested . . . .

The list goes on.

Death Watch

for David

Vultures begin their gathering rituals.
Even before the event has seized the body.
And the man who has become blind
by the oncoming confrontation
does not see how they ease their way
towards his slowed form.
How they nit-pick. Impatient. Pecking.
Curiously scanning his line of muscle.
Testing his resistance
from their precariously secure distances.
Measuring his powers of self-defense
with their stalemate of calculated strategies.
Timing their limping target, aiming to disarm.
To seize vulnerable tissue. Hungry
to dissrupt, scavenge fresh meat.

But the man who no longer cares
has prematurely vacated occupancy
of all he claimed his worldly kingdom.
His mind a wandering labyrinth.
Unable to remember previous minutes,
precious seconds of a former life.
Trying to decipher through oceans of confusion
to the next overdose of prescribed relief.
Anxious to sleep.
Escape to the only path from suffering
like a warden, sentenced to capital pain.

While the vultures prepare their anticipated feast
of this man who once became master of himself.
Whose mother heard her womb cry
abandoned and angry from their hunger.
This man who fought poverty like a warrior,
sculptured his life like a jewel,
sported and dined like a connoisseur,
worked two jobs,
loved himself as he learned to believe,

overcoming his cross,
conquering the inner battle, fear of self.

Now vultures circle in their death dance
with numerous faces.
Bureaucrats shifting responsibility,
shuffling lives into despair
with small promises mimicking concern,
motivated by their fat accounts,
unable to diagnose their symptomatic insularities,
false healers under guise of cure.

Even faces of dry relatives gritting camouflaged smiles
in grand theatrical displays.

While the man has ceased all outside desire,
forfeited ownership of designer clothes.
Even the sunset has become irrelevant,
replaced by interplay of sores and seizures.
Betrayed by his own memory,
now an enemy full of tricks.

The vultures perform their ritual gathering
long before the final event.
Grabbing. Tearing. Claiming.
At war with each other over his valuable residue.
While the man who has become numb,
slips away. A helpless child
groping into the unknown
with all that is left of his dignity.
Until finally, the few who loved him pray
for his new-found peace.

Because Life Is A Bitch

for Jorge Soto

We mourn not for death
but for life,
your premature sacrifice,
a delicate treasure in our history museum,
a cutting machete, your pages of precision,
photographic inscriptions in docu-real,
a cursed vision that screams a surreal line
sculptured to completion.

We mourn ourselves
who are left to fill the deep space you carved,
foundations of seedling, water rotted rainforest
pushed to hysterical insanity
by that loose backbone of ambivalence,
like hunger sick hawks,
building nests between stone mentalities,
fighting the continuous turbulence of discovering self.

We mourn your vision, our eyes exposing naked truth,
revealing her jagged mirror's edge, bloody and treacherous.
A fated survival.

We mourn our memory, your Cabio Sile chant
circumcising our eardrums in fierce bata,
signaling war in the battlefield of mind
where music is the healer of sins.

We mourn our salt-dried tears, blood filled
from the nail that claimed you,
that forced you down,
that empowered the magic of your feathered pen,
stripping all untruths from the clear focus of your canvas.

That once Soto passed through here
sharing definitions, birth to our voices,
achieving victory, even before death.

Jorge, who touched us

with spiritual jewels recovered from the whirlwind,
a catabolic fuse, slow, but hot
like a passing time bomb.

Poema Para La Muerte

When death approaches
speaking in straightforward tongue,
its dialect polarized by the promise of blood,
words weighing meaning, releasing ignorance,
its method centered in surprise attack,
changing your life path,
forcing your rebirth from the ashes of a brilliant fire,
burning away your old clothing,
replacing it with new style,
a luminous coat, empowered with knowledge of yourself,
powerless but to continue
on a road cleared of sticky thorns, impenetrable bush,
in a forward direction
that closes and swallows itself behind you.

When death visits your sanctuary
you cannot ignore its staring face,
nor turn to walk away,
nor deceive yourself into thinking it is not there.
Its inescapable odor violates your senses,
forcing you to entertain it,
an unwelcomed dinner guest, rude and boastful,
who eats up all your food,
leaving nothing for the rest of your family
as it dines on the life force of your soul.

You try to save your children.
You hide them under your mantle.
You disguise them behind masks
and camouflage their hair in rosebuds.
You teach them to speak a different language,
hoping they will not reveal any secrets.
You hold onto them constantly,
and cry when you have to let them go.
But sooner or later you have to.
And you pray at your altar for their safe return.
Knowing that death does not discriminate,
does not care

about sex, age, political affiliation, or religious inclination.
It doesn't matter what divine power you speak to,
or how many candles you light a week,
or if you don't at all,
or whether you care about the world,
or are indifferent to it.

Sooner or later, death presents itself
like it always comes, a thief, a beggar of sacrifice,
murderous.

Scattering your life.
Charging you with the responsibility of making it work.
Accepting what was never planned or expected.

So you deal with it anyway. Alone or together,
however you have to, because you're a survivor.

When death follows you
like an armed hunter
setting loaded shackles
and all manner of weapons against you,
tracking your movements with mad obsession,
you dare not sleep, or look away from your door,
hoping it will bypass your home like misguided locust,
its hunger detoured by the sudden uprising of a scented
     wind.

You try to silence your sounds,
darken your lights, become invisible,
until you hear your heart, a deafening storm,
rising from your sweat,
sending signals to reveal your identity,
illuminating your location,
forcing you to realize that the only path to silence
is to submit to your fears,
until you become fearless, knowing that God,
the saints, your ancestors, and guardian angel
walk always with you.

Through death the goddess, Aché Oya, speaks,
Madama of the cemetery,
Señora with feet lodged between two worlds.
The right in logical reality, basic and practical.
The left reaching to the other side of the mind,

inside environments of dreams and spiritual messages.

She says that all is well,
guiding turbulence with direct intentions.
That everything happens for reasons,
detours on the crossroads,
sent blessings
transforming us into new day purified,
where the horizon of tomorrow is the promise of begin-
     nings,
and today's pain becomes a sacrifice
of bruises changed to kisses, each one,
profound universes of candles aflame.

Who Is Going To Tell Me?

for España

España, golden father of my ancestors,
who captured my mother as slave, stripped her naked,
plowed treasures from her shores.

To you, who claims hills most green, wine most sweet,
Spanish most precise, devotion most fervent.
Whose structured guitar the most elegant
and flamenco the most graceful.

To you, initiate
whose model blessed this western land
where Columbus recovered his wealthy Caribbean key
opening door to Española—Santo Domingo,
giving birth to the history of a million shames,
where the names of kings, imamus, caciques and warlords
were secrets disguised, abolished,
dissolved into myriads of bloodlines,
claiming invisible records, unwritten,
stolen from the lucious continents.

To you, father of my father,
whose table graced our tobacco fields,
whose whip increased the abundance of our sweet cane,
grinding sweat from roots to water your rose garden of thorns.
Whose court inspired our danzón, corrido, and gracious bomba,
giving rise to a new African drumbeat—the flight of the ball
    and chain,
creating the formulation of new words, esclavo, cimarrón,
    slave, rebel.

To you, who hides in mountains of golden courtly seals
inside handwrought manuscripts from the age of Ferdinand.
On whose gilded pages are inscribed
the names of my great grandmothers?
Inside what illustrations are located
the landmark homes of my great grandfathers?
On the maps of which islands

rest their simple graves where I may pay hommage to my
    ancestors?
In whose kingly court
did my great grand-aunt wet nurse the master's brats?
Perhaps a future uncle, or slightly remembered landowner.
And which of my grand cousins were teachers?
Masters of their craft, respected noblemen, and women of
    wisdom?
In whose library will I find their books? Tales of their lives?
On which ships did my captured relatives sail?
At which ports did their feet first land?
To which continents were relatives dispersed?
To Brazil, Venezuela, Argentina, Bolivia,
Colombia, Costa Rica, Cuba, Ecuador,
Peru, the Dominican Republic, Uruguay, Jamaica,
Haiti, the Caribbean Antilles, the Mexican Coast, Panamá,
Yucatan, the thirteen colonies, New Orleans, Virginia,
South Carolina, Mississippi, Alabama, Nueva York?
To you, singing canticles of Spanish kings of Barcelona,
where Maximillian danced his Roman feast of world con-
    quest,
forming the anguished tears of Goya,
forging the broken cubes of Picasso,
giving substance to the cries of García Lorca.

In all your illustrious bounty hides a legacy denied.
Yet, not one line of testimony to this truth of shame,
nor one admission of guilt, nor humble apology,
nor effort to replace what was defiled, dismembered.

To you, España, prize of Europe,
host to the colonized West,
solicitor of rich ports,
seducer of saintly Indians,
golden father of my ancestors, who captured my mother as
    slave,
stripped her naked, plowed treasures from her shores.

I want to know your future.

What new paintings will be created on whose walls?
Whose names will emerge in which new brilliant journals?
What melodies will evolve from our mixings?
In whose gardens will we water our visions?

I want to know
who will decide our fate?
You, or I, or WE together?

Will I be free to discover my own path?
Uncover a new journey no one else has known?
Designing my life spaces in my own natural colors,
tropical parades of evergreens,
caribbean blue seas, sand surfaces,
and mountain-rain-banana-leaf horizons.

I want to know.

Who is going to tell me?

Puerto Rican Discovery #6, Lodestar

for Suzana

Aquarian eyed vision just ahead of tomorrow
where eagles gather to invite the sun.
Caciques in pow-wow over the fate of their children
and one bright star more powerful than all,
by nature of location,
the cause and effect of night and day,
the hand that chops away the sugar cane,
that picks the cotton and coffee harvest,
resemebling the world
from the womb of wombed-man,
that belongs to the mind of the Eternal Deity,
that bows on its knees to pray,
that the chains around its wrist be set free—
that the chains be set free—
be set free—set free ....

Open Memo To The Congressional Appropiations
Committee And The Military Department Of Defense

To Whom It Does Concern:

Could we please have just one space flight,
one nine-million dollar adventure into the great breath,
so that we could divide the loaves and fishes
and put 900 more people to work for a year.

Or could we please have one nuclear missile,
so we can difuse it, sell the used parts
for one-point-ten billion worth of more than just
rice krispies breakfast-lunch-dinners.

What if we could exchange an M-1 rifle for a solar reflector
so that our building could have heat all the time,
not wait for avaricious gun-toting landlords
to remember to call the oil company tomorrow
for the child next door with pneumonia today.

We would even accept a leftover bomber,
or one two-million dollar high tech space suit,
however patronizing it may seem,
or a decommissioned aircraft carrier to relieve tight housing
      problems.

Its not much, is it?
When you add it up, pull together the sum total
of the four billion dollars-a-day catastrophy fantasy,
the whole is worse than its parts.

So to continue our list,
could you please refund on our next tax return
the difference between the limousines you drive,
and the tokens we do not have
to build our nation strong.

                              Signed,
                              The People of the Rest of the World

Point Of Information

for a Cuban comrade

Permiso, compañero,
but I have to disagree

about the importance of political economics
over that of a poem.

However you see the difference,
I do not.

Between the balance of nations
exists the economy of words.

From these seeds the future is formed,
bearing in mind

that only through progressive dialogue
is direction ever found.

Anonymous Apartheid

There is a stranger in our house
who looks half blind at us,
does not know our name,
assumes our earth is flat,
wraps a ball and chain around our tired legs,
barricades our windows with formless visions,
illusions of no consequence.

This stranger thinks we are alley cats, purring
in heat for violent attentions,
feeds us day-old fish and dead meat,
leaves our fruit basket empty,
does not speak our language, wear our colors,
nor understand the soul of these tender thoughts.

The stranger upsets our garden,
turning over seeds of potential into desert soil,
laying waste the promise of life's harvest,
denied, for no better reason than greed,
chopping down innocent buds to feed
their wealth of scavengers, and thieves,
growing fat from the treasures we are.

This stranger steals us from our mother,
separates us from our brothers and sisters,
does not listen to our million crying petitions,
cuts off our rebelious tongues,
laughs when our tears fall on stone,
orders us to kneel, though we refuse.

Each day the stranger drinks a nectar of blood at high noon,
wears clothing spun from blood,
worships a heathen blood god made of gold,
destroys the covenant of humanity
for the sake of a synthetic blood mirror, cracked,
tarnished quicksilver, ungrounded and formless,
traveling a broken spiral of blood.

This stranger lives here uninvited,

an unwelcomed alien ravaging us in gluttonous consumma-
    tion,
throwing a soiled shroud over our altar,
expecting us to accept a life of disgrace.
Yet, we refuse.

There is a ruthless stranger in our house
who has no voice of its own,
mimics our words in crude scorn,
suggests we are low, worthless, incompetent,
grinning at itself
while we are held hostage in a doomed drama
where act one lasts more than five hundred years,
in plots of bigoted abuse,
dialogues of racial condescension, poverty,
transitions of rapes, muggings, lynchings,
scenes of jailhouse tortures and hangings,
life sentences to minimum security housing projects.

There is a stranger in our house
plundering our womb,
stealing our newborn with a dry knife,
drug-thirsty for their blood,
bargains in exchange for their lives,
tells us to throw away our weapons, love one another,
rejecting our religion,
forcing us to sell our worth,
poisoning the rich center of our spiritual essence,
speaking the lecherous tongue of split truth.

Yet we refuse, and will continue to refuse,
along with our planetary relatives who also refuse
this stranger in our house
who has no face.

Fighting Demons

for South Africa

What is the difference between here and there?
Between what is seen and the elusive face?
Fascism or imperialism,
South Africa, New York,
South Bronx, Soweto, Harlem, East Harlem, Namibia,
Lower East Side, Sharpville, Williamsburg, Watts, Johan-
 nesburg.

What is the difference?
Between sunburnt hands knocking vainly on the blind doors
 of apartheid?
That haven of disunity that forgets how it was molded from
 the dirt,
descended from the rich clay wombed mother,
that bore a continent through slavery,
here or there denied its inheritence,
here or there in iron ore chains,
stripped from the same sacred vessels, plucked from the
 same mountain breast
that nourished the birth of all creation,
that brought forth Yoruba incantations for life,
the science and precision of Mayan astrology,
the wisdom and passion of the Cherokee,
that filled the sky of the children of the Hopi,
offering hommage to a sungod where Arawak rivers of fire
 mountain blood
dance out a heartbeat for the darkness and the ocean of a
 million coquí.

Here? There? What is the difference?
When hunger thrives from unemployed nightmares created
 on a neon trip
down madison avenue by mercenaries of the inner soul,
paying first class rates just above the poverty line?

What is the difference in the name of the bank
that funds the weapons of racism?

That suppresses nations of builders into limbo/drug/ depres-
    sion/regression,
oppression on a master scale?

South Africa. New York. What is the difference in the face
    of greed?
How does it construct its smile from the burning bones of
    Vietnamese families,
or the screams of a million martyred students in a stadium
    filled horror
that witnessed the slashing of the poet's tongue, the murder
    of Víctor Jara,
the hanging of Benjamin Meloise?

South Africa. New York.
Chile. Guatemala. Puerto Rico. Nicaragua.
Ireland. Ethiopia. El Salvador. Panama.
Kent State. Attica. Beirut.
What is the difference in the perfect equation?
That brings food to every table in a banquet of sharing and
    dignity applied?
That writes this book of truth. That difuses the bomb of
    oblivion.
That ignites the fires of compassion. That lights the torches
    of liberation.
To set South Africa free.
That will set South Africa free.

—That MUST set South Africa free.

Puerto Rican Discovery #7, In The Eye Of The Storm

for Vieques and Culebra

There are no feelings a hurricane can sense,
only power to consume an unholy bread.

No mouth. Its thunder is a facade
speaking from a machine
spitting out a regimented garble of formulae at billion-per-
    second rates.

It has no eyes.
Does not know how to watch the changeable wind through
    steadfast trees,
or the steady rise of mountains through years.

Its belly is empty.
Contains tumultuous revolutions.
Chaos broken from bits and pieces of severed struggles.
Leaving heaped trails of death.
Making whores of innocent newborn.
Victims of each pure feeling.

Braintwister

for Cielo Azul

Intelligent life
is often stupid
how we open our mouths
have nothing to say
try to write love poems
are caught choking
or bent over money
forgetting how to speak
teeth falling out
chicken bones in our throats
nostrils inflamed
a trail of smoke
following the path of our tongues.

3

Batarumba Autonomy

Rumba Amiga, Amiga

para Irma

Eh, aché, mi hermana, eh, aché.
El sol te brinda un saludo
a tu belleza presencia
andando como reina
en su propia casa.

Aché, mi hermana,
como hermana de todos.
Con tu amor grande
cubriendo el mundo,
acariciando vida
en gran celebración.

Aché, compañera,
acompañada de confirmación.
Tu ambiente espiritual brilla
con tu esperanza profunda
magnificando sentidos sencillos
de familia hasta familia,
de persona hasta persona,
de mujer hasta amiga.

Aché, amiga, aché.
Tu pasion es un lindo baile
al lado tu mesa blanca
que sirve un trópico fresco
de madamitas y santos
que diario te siguen
con brazos muy fuertes,
corazones puros,
acentos afilados,
puños finos,
en tu claridad siguiendo atrás de Dios.

Gringolandia

for Martín Espada

How I love to listen to north american intellectuals.
The way they utilize language, brutalize communication,
glibly flip speech from the tips of their flying tongues,
spontaneous maneuverings
on the precise order of perfection.
Always knowing. Absolutely aware
of the exact format of correctness.
Never failing. Never mistaking
a lie for anything not resembling it.
Commanding the copywright of thought communication
with presumptuous ownership.
Definitively clear on the ingredients of the perfect poem,
the metamorphosis of the superlative metaphor,
the inharmonious insistence on
control-domination-instinctive-twitch.

How I love to listen.
Remind myself there is more to the world.
The whole of it.
The multinational ethnicity of it.
The many prismed expression of it.
The strength and struggle of it.
How I have learned to grow from it.
To love and praise myself from it.
To let the life force flow from it.
To be in tune as one to it.

Perceive the face of death whenever/wherever it stares at
        me.
Then establish the rhythm of counterbalance,
the offbeat note of discovery at the crossroads
where montuno comes alive.

Affirmations #3, Take Off Your Mask

Study the face behind it.
The óne that has no flesh or bones.
The one that feels what the universe feels.

Take off the mask. Discard it.
Useless shell that it is.
An old skin. A cover.
Subject to weather distortions.

See for yourself
the you inside no one else can see.

In The Ring

for Marvin Félix Camillo

When a boxer answers the bell,
his body a tight fighting machine,
concentration focused to serious business,
a controlled serpent coiled to attack,
positioning stance square opponent,
deciphering through the shower of superficial jabs,
anticipating the decisive moment of power,
a fine-tuned double-edged lightening strike,
timing the ultimate t.k.o.,
targeting aim to a clean finish,
claiming the prize on the bloody stage of victory,

taking all the punches like a champ.

Black Notes And "You Do Something To Me"

for Gerry González and The Fort Apache Band

Jazz—jazzy jass juice,
just so smooth,
so be-bop samba blue to sweet bump black.
So slip slide back to mama black—
to mamaland base black.
Don't matter could be bronx born basic street black.
Or white ivory piano coast negro dunes bembé black.
Mezclando manos in polyrhythm sync to fingers,
to keys, to valves, to strings, to sticks,
to bells, to skins, to YEAH black.
Bringin' it home black.
The bad Fort Apache tan olive brown beat black.
Bringin' it all the way up fast black.
Flyin' across Miles 'n Sony,
across John, Rhasaan 'n Monk's '81,
across Dizzy blue conga Jerry horn,
'n básico Andy mo-jo black.
Across Nicky's campana timbaleando tumbao black.
'N Dalto's multi-octave chords with all those keys black.
Those multifarious dimensional openings
playin' loud—soft—hard—cold—slow—'n—suavecito black.
Playin' it runnin'—jumpin'—cookin'—greasin'—'n—smokin'
    black.
Playin' it mellow, yeah mellow,
makin' it mean somethin' black.
Makin' it move, rockin' round black.
Walk with it, talk with it, wake the dead with it black.
Turnin' it out, touchin' the sky with it black.
Shakin' it suave, shakin' it loose,
shakin' it che-ché-que-re black.
Season it, sugar it, lingerin', lullaby black.
Livin' it, ALIVE BLACK!
Always lovin' it—Yeah!

Jazz.
How I love your sweet soul sounds.

Yeah,
how I love how you love me.
Yeah, how I love that deep black thang ...

                    ... "You do so well" ...

From The Ferrybank

for J. Strawder

Who are we this moment? We, who focus
our nearsighted vision on reflections
from a gleaming riverbank, waiting for clear
waters to arrive in switching
undercurrents. We, who balance giant
steps on a sinking sanded shore, giving
grace to our swallowed presence slipping
through lucid tides.

Who are we, on this day, crying
for rebirth. The reawakened seed, born
from the holy tree where one is brother
to all brothers, sister
to all sisters. We who watch the gilded
ships float through the mysterious
river, offering our simple bowl
of rice to all of heaven, singing
inbetween our dreary despair, evolving
occult melodies from our work songs, casting
our sights across an ocean of changing
horizons, vying for attentions of mighty
kings, majestic queens, guided
by the shimmering light of a distant
solitary star rising from the tail of darkness.
We who come from mountains where
trees stretch across an unending
sky, where air thins to a burning
delicacy served on a spiritual buffet, abundant
and fresh, newly formed and moist.

Who are we today, now, waiting
on shores of fulfillment for a promised
cargo carrying varieties of fish chased
by eagles gliding on and over an unstable
surface, plucking survival and nourishment
from a turbulent sea, hungering
after an unspoken peace, starved for the delicious

beauty of seasoned dignity, ravenous
for love's light in the mirrored sight
of a remembrance, where an amorphous hurricane
plays against a softly swaying samba, following
the calculated flow of waves, breaking, dissolving
into the voluminous ocean, spread
across the seven seas, discovered
and revived anew in the thunderstorm.

Resurrections

We come to the dance,
our legs in pain,
muscles protruding, swollen
red from battle,
bodies limping distortion scars,
eyes veiled with inner rage,
words hot as sun.

We come to the dance
parched for miracle drops of holy water,
cures for self and the world's diseases
embedded in the unseen.

We, the lonely victims, come
deaf from the madness,
desperate for the naked sounds
of rainbow waterfalls,
wanting to drink,
partake in the treasured secrets of our ancestors.

Oshun's Love Poem

The first time I saw you on the mountain,
scouting through the luscious forest,
hunting with your golden bow
erect towards heaven.
Brush full, blue sky and yellow paint
across your warrior face,
your hunter's fierce stare, obsessed
like a mad priest.
I watched you visible like sunlight
that flows through the pattern of the trees,
two seconds before I fell
to the power of your silent arrow,
unsuspecting and wounded,
unable to disengage the snare
or break that heavy chain
locking my soul to yours,
as you held me tight and secure,
hand and feet tied limp across your back,
cross wrapped over your arm,
helpless against the curve of your neck,
teased by the wind-blown wave of your hair,
intoxicated by your sweat, rising,
steaming in the heat,
with its perfume of seduction
drugging me in transcendental suspension and vicious fan-
     tasy,
where you lay me bare
in an eternal nightly drama,
stripping me of my skin,
attaching my feathers
along the arched edges of your bow,
like an object of beauty
graced by your possession,
consumed by your touch,
ignited by your tongue,
fire through your blood,
full as moon,

as water filling your thirsty bowl,
nourishing the green stem of your turquoise flower,
as I become moist and drunk,
made fresh from your nectar,

cooled in the shadow of your powerful brilliance.

Affirmations #4 ·

I seek the brilliant sun appearing through dark horizons
rising over this empty canvas,
creating poems from the ashes of charred histories
teaching me to walk by deciphering futures
that sip the wine of life from a gemstone goblet,
focusing the loaded tip of this superfluous pen
from a ragged surface into a balanced line of dignity
opening doors to the unspoken,
the lodestar following its source,
the changing river flowing towards the ocean,
the restless sea moved by the sway of the moon.

I seek poems that rise from the ashes
wherein lies the path of completion,
becoming master of myself.

All praises. All praises. All praises.

Padrino

for John Mason

Round sleeping-moon face
from where watchful seers interpret visions
sent by caring saints,
viewing into realms where we are blind.
Choosing to guide our steep awkward climbing
with their buoyant hands holding us secure
over the bottomless pit
where we are conquered by a skilled magician's faith,
head crowned by magic herbal wreath,
crimson berries bedded in fresh mint,
infusing sacred words through holy breath
that clears soul-clouding cataracts of illusion,
setting our spirits free
with barely a touch and gentle incantation,
causing our rebirth,
to become blessed fruit, made sweet
and ripe for offering in the final ritual
where we return to the house of our ancestors,
a grand mansion full of infinite rooms
under a chandelier of stars
pulsating precise cosmic music,
vibrations consuming darkness,
revealing what is greater within ourselves
where we live as native children
riding on tall vine swings,
suspended from the high branches of an old wisdom tree
in the mystical playground of our Great Grandfather's garden.

Bautizo

for Brunie

Early Brooklyn morning
Padrino counsels initiates,
new children into his house,
spiritual survivors reclaimed from a pilfered legacy.

Silent and anxious
the iabos shed old clothes
that hang on and grip like tight skins
of solid lead shackles. A burden
heavier than their ability to resist.
Acknowledging need to align
cumbersome physical being with Divine power,
diminishing the weight,
implementing knowledge of metaphysical chemistry,
the natural combustion of kinetic earth, composed
and refined in the transcendental laboratory of mind.

Full of aché,
Babalorisha invokes the ancestors,
family of one-hundred-thousand names,
to join this rebirth,
sing and feast in prodigal victory,
reaffirming linkage
to bloodlines woven like luminous veils
over walls and windows of their souls,
opening to reveal the precious landscapes
and inherited panoramas of our connected intelligence.

Life Is A Journey

... on a greyhound bus
arriving at your destination
like a young girl, self-conscious,
worried about her looks.

At the station the bus pulls up.
Waiting in line are her ancestors
wearing blue and white ritual clothes,
their faces long and serious.

She thinks she has to get new clothes.

Ocha

Crawling through the ground,
hidden and covered in slime,
begins the metamorphosis of the butterfly.

Almost at the point of death,
dormant, frozen in its prison,
asleep and unaware of its future,
until its casing presses tight,
breathless against its skin
as it stirs in its initiation,
pushing at the walls that hold
like a sealed coffin,
finding need for its own rebellion,
heaving its liberation song with calculated force,
a ritual guided,
pulled forward through a slight crack
like beacon barely sighted over a stormy sea,
like the tender promise of a lover's kiss
after annihilation in the war of loneliness,
stretching out slowly,
limb after untrained limb,
emerging through its birth canal,
disoriented and dizzy,
unfolding one fan wing, then another,
to dry, visible and free over the fields,
revealing qualities of the prismatic universe
that powers it to flight,
to feast in the eternal garden,
empowered by itself
with beauty blazing mantle adorning its back,
head crowned luminous,
blessed by the eccentric wind,
blowing magnetically towards the midday sky,

receiving its final gift:
a left-sided wing,
invisible, perfumed,
trailing a direct spiral into heaven.

101st Poem For My Husband

So hungry,

I will take whatever you give me.
Make it ours.
Powerful works of art,
real and whole.

Even if it is my secret.

Even if you never know.

Even if these shallow words
are all I have.